IMAGES
of America

TALLASSEE

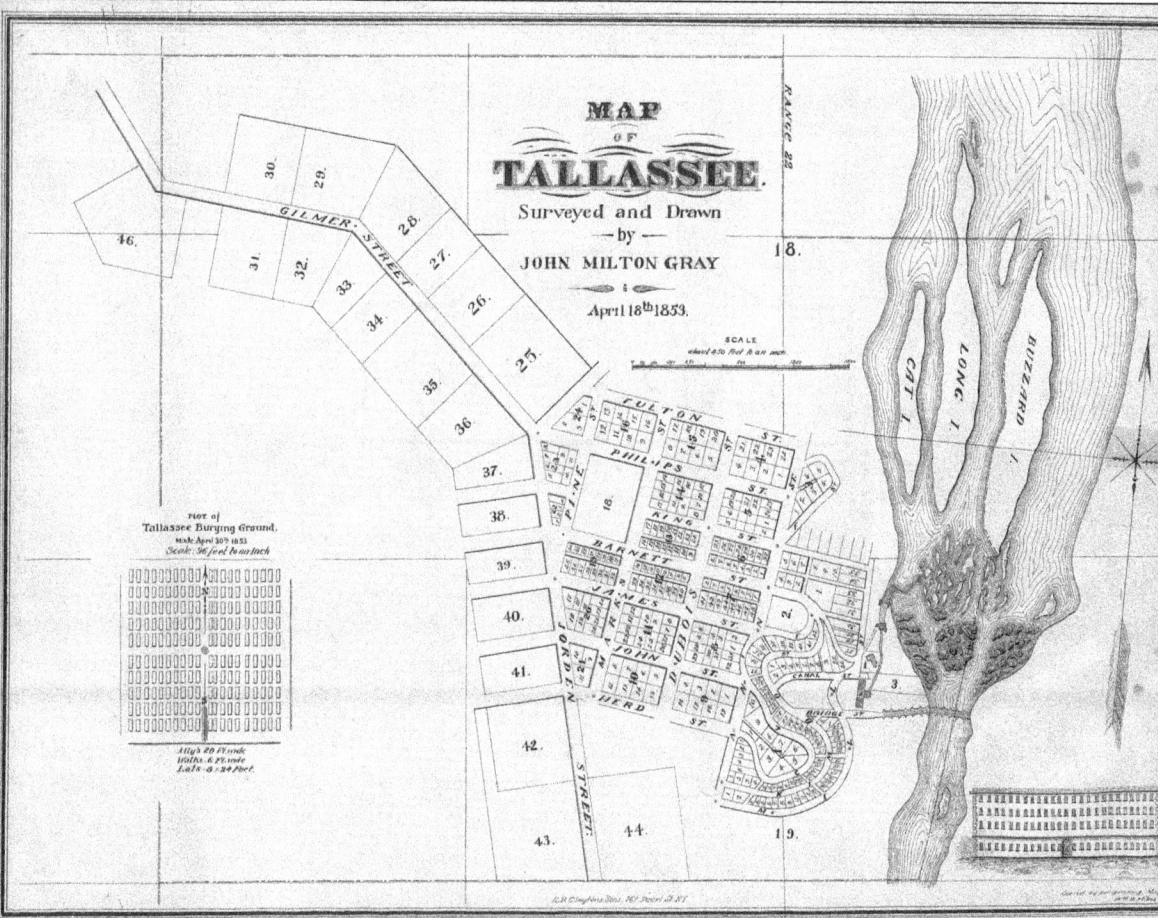

The first map of Tallassee, drawn by John Milton Gray in 1853, shows the blocks and streets, the 1844 and 1852 Tallassee Mills, the Tallapoosa River, and the Tallassee burying grounds. The map was authorized by Thomas Meriwether Barnett (1785–1857), the father of Tallassee. (Courtesy Talisi Historical Preservation Society.)

IMAGES
of America

TALLASSEE

William E. Goss and Karren Pell

ARCADIA
PUBLISHING

Published by Arcadia Publishing
Charleston, South Carolina

Library of Congress Catalog Card Number: 2007937248

For all general information contact Arcadia Publishing at:
Telephone 843-853-2070
Fax 843-853-0044
E-mail sales@arcadiapublishing.com
For customer service and orders:
Toll-Free 1-888-313-2665

Visit us on the Internet at www.arcadiapublishing.com

The Neal Brothers' photograph shows the Tallassee Falls Manufacturing Company in the 1890s on the west side of the Tallapoosa River. (Courtesy THPS.)

CONTENTS

ACKNOWLEDGMENTS

The majority of the photographs contained in this book were taken from the Talisi Historical Preservation Society (THPS) archives; therefore, the authors wish to thank the society and those who have contributed photographs and support to the THPS.

The authors also take this opportunity to express their appreciation to Florian Web of Auburn Montgomery Information and Technical Services for his skill and patience. Other Auburn Montgomery services and individuals who gave us invaluable assistance are as follows: Jason Kneip, Special Collections librarian; the Auburn Montgomery Library (AUM Library); and Dr. Craig Sheldon.

Our thanks for contributions of photographs and information go to the First Baptist Church Montgomery, Ralph Foster, Tommy and Jane Baker Bryant, Carole King, Edward Pattillo, and Timothy Henderson. Credit and appreciation is also due to James H. Boatwright, John Andrew Herren, Frederica Dobbs Melton, Harold (Pete) Cottle, Patricia and Reginald Anthony, Jeff Parker, Billy Thompson, Betty Blakely Mason, Paula Eller Castleberry, Peggy Stanfield Landers, Bennie Little, Betty Watts Diamond, the Tallassee City Board of Education, and the Tallassee First Baptist Church.

Thanks go to Sherry and Linn Boswell for giving Karren the idea to contact Arcadia Publishing. We were fortunate to have two editors; our appreciation goes to Jami Sheppard for helping us get started and to Brooksi Hudson for helping us get finished.

INTRODUCTION

It can be argued that Tallassee's story began approximately 280 million years ago when the tectonic plates of the North American and African continents collided. The massive impact created the Appalachian Mountains, the "fall line" where those fabled peaks end, and the great waterfalls that both define and divide the town of Tallassee.

Tallassee's recorded human history began when the Muskogee/Creek Indians built the first settlement by the great falls and called it Talisi. Noted on maps from the 1700s, the town stood for many years at the mouth of Euphaubee Creek where it meets the Tallapoosa River, about three miles from the current Tallassee.

In 1798, Indian agent Benjamin Hawkins described the falls, the timbered hillside, and the riverbed rock, and made his prophetic observation concerning these assets: "sufficient for the building of a large city . . . and the river is convenient . . . for mills on an extensive scale."

Close by, Talisi's "sister city," Tukabahchi, was a younger Creek settlement and the last great capital of the Creek Confederacy. Tecumseh's famous visit to Tukabahchi in 1811 was the spark that kindled war and, in the end, reduced to ashes the Native American's claim to the land the white settlers would settle and, in their turn, call "Tallassee."

An intriguing character in Tallassee's story, Barent DuBois, arrived in the 1820s and became the first white settler and the founder of modern Tallassee. He married a Creek woman named Milly Reed. Prior to the removal of the Creek Indians, DuBois made use of his government connections and Milly's tribal affiliation, and by 1840, they owned 2,092 acres.

Tallassee's next chapter began when two white settlements were founded after the removal of the Native Americans. The first settlement was below where the present town now stands and was called, obviously in reference to the Creek town, "Tallassee" or "Tallassee Town," and is referred to as "Old Town." In 1844, Barent and Milly DuBois sold the land for the site of Tallassee's first textile mill, the second built in Alabama, to Thomas Meriwether Barnett and William M. Marks. The mill was known as Barnett and Marks. The economic and social focus shifted to the textile mill, stifling the growth of Old Town; it was deserted by 1863. Barnett, who is affectionately referred to as the father of the current city, named the settlement "Tallassee" after the old Native American town whose residents had so recently been forced to leave for western lands.

As Tallassee's story continued, planters raised cotton, the mills prospered, and Tallassee grew. By 1852, a second 4-story mill rose along the banks of the Tallapoosa. The town flourished—homes were built high on the hill overlooking the river, a blacksmith shop kept horses and wagons moving, a cotton gin supported the mill, and gristmills ground meal for Tallassee's tables.

Leading up to the Civil War, the people living in Tallassee were not as focused on the issue of slavery and secession as their contemporaries. Most of Tallassee's residents had left small farms to work in the mills. They had never owned slaves and did not have the same heated sentiments regarding slavery and secession as did the Tallapoosa River planters. Nonetheless, when war came, the men of Tallassee fought for Alabama and the Southern cause; more than 100 volunteered for service in the Confederate army. However, service options for men in Tallassee were not limited to wearing a uniform and shooting a gun; those who made the uniforms and guns were considered equally valuable. Tallassee's industrial contributions were so important that the Confederate government passed a special law exempting men working in the mills and arms factories from the Enrollment Act. During the Civil War, Tallassee became an important supply center for the Confederacy. The mills, then known as Barnett, Micou, and Company, produced cloth for uniforms, cots, and tents. The old mill was converted into an armory that manufactured carbines. Homes were built for army supervisors, and food was raised to supply the workers and supervisors.

Tradition holds that Union forces twice attempted to find and destroy the armory and, most probably, Tallassee as well. The Union's main problem involved Tallassee's rural location. However, tales abound featuring a multitude of characters, the Tallassee Home Guard, Gen. Nathan Bedford Forrest, a faulty map, and a Union commander who refused to follow directions. The different tales always end the same: Union soldiers never reached Tallassee, and so the town boasts the only Confederate armory standing today.

After the Civil War, the soldiers who returned to Tallassee found life a little easier than in some parts of the South during Reconstruction as the local economy was based more on the mills than on the plantations. As the years passed, the mills endured some economic ups and downs, but basically, Tallassee remained the small town by the great falls. Its sons and daughters worked in the mills, attended the schools, raised families, and shared fellowship and worship in the churches.

At the end of the 1800s, Tallassee became a boomtown—the epitome of the "New South." The mills had undergone reorganization and expansion, were recognized as the South's most impressive textile complex, and had a new name: Tallassee Falls Manufacturing Company. The new Textile Mill No. 2 was four stories built from the blue-gray granite of the Tallapoosa riverbed. At that time, the building was reputed to be the largest textile plant in the world made of stone (most mills were built of brick). By wagons and trains, textile products bearing the name "Tallassee Mills" were shipped from the textile mills of Tallassee to the growing industrial cities of the South and to Europe and Asia.

The beginning of a new century started a new chapter in Tallassee's story. The Tallassee Falls Manufacturing Company became part of the Mount Vernon–Woodberry Cotton Duck Company. The company was a conglomerate with a home office in Baltimore, Maryland, and plants in various parts of the country. The new owners brought in new ideas, and Tallassee became less isolated. As a part of the Textile Mill No. 2 expansion in 1898, a new mill village on the east side of the Tallapoosa was built for workers. A large, two-story company store was also built in East Tallassee. In addition to offering general merchandise for mill workers, the building housed a drugstore, a post office, and a lodge hall.

However, the improvements did not bring about the expected revenue. By 1914, the boom period was fading, and the residents of Tallassee began to feel negative effects from the mills' financial problems. Wages were reduced, and employees' homes were not maintained; the mill property also went into decline. Some workers and residents left for greener pastures and never returned.

The economic downturn was reversed when World War I began on July 28, 1914. The Tallassee Mills increased production to meet the need for cotton duck and canvas for army tents and cots. Many young men from Tallassee served in the armed forces. Throughout the war, the people of Tallassee who worked in the mills supported the war effort both in the field and in the mills.

But the war in Europe was not the only conflict Tallassee was involved in during the first part of the 20th century. In 1916 the mills, then known as the Mount Vernon–Woodberry Cotton Duck Company, fought a court battle with the Alabama Power Company, a state utility. In 1911, the Alabama Light and Power Company approached the owners of the mills with plans to build a dam above the great falls at Tallassee to generate energy for public use. At that time, the Mount Vernon–Woodberry Cotton Duck Company owned not only the mills and the land where they stood, but also most of the town of Tallassee, the right-of-way to the falls, and the dam that was then in place over the falls. The mills and the power company were not able to negotiate a settlement, and a legal battle ended up in the Supreme Court of the United States. In a landmark decision, Justice Oliver Wendell Holmes decided in favor of Alabama Light and Power and so ushered in the age of the public sector in Tallassee and Alabama as a whole. Although the mills lost that battle, in the final analysis, both the mills and the town of Tallassee benefited from the decision because the new dam provided increased energy for the mills and made electricity available for the residents of Tallassee.

On Armistice Day, November 11, 1918, the Tallassee Mills stopped at 4:45 p.m. to celebrate the end of World War I. The church bells rang, and the mill whistles blew. That night, a torchlight parade wound through Tallassee to celebrate the victory.

Almost a year later to the date, after several days of continuous rain, the Tallapoosa River reached flood stage. On December 9, 1919, the rising waters collapsed the Montgomery Light and Water Company dam about four miles above Tallassee. The waters broke free, creating a wave that crashed into the Tallassee Mills dam, destroying it and the bridge. The water-supply facilities for the mills and the town of Tallassee were damaged, and water had to be rationed. The railroad was out of service for several months. Most of the machinery in the mills' powerhouse was ruined. Slowly and steadily the town began to recover. A year later, a new permanent bridge spanned the Tallapoosa River.

After the great flood, extensive repairs and changes were instituted both at the mills and in the mill housing, including installing electricity and running water in the houses. In 1924, the Alabama Power Company took over the Montgomery Light and Water Power Company's dam and power plant at Tallassee and immediately rebuilt the damaged dam and power plant. The increased power contributed to the increased prosperity Tallassee enjoyed in the 1920s.

Downtown Tallassee was a hub of business activity in the 1920s. With a luxury hotel, busy textile mills, and prosperous retail establishments, the 1920s were a fun time in Tallassee's story. Construction began on Thurlow Dam on April 5, 1928; built on top of the old Tallassee Mills dam. It was completed on December 31, 1930. Thurlow Dam created Lake Talisi with a shoreline of six miles and an area of 574 acres. Today the power generated by the chain of Martin, Yates, Thurlow, and Harris dams, all on the Tallapoosa River, supplies electricity not only to Tallassee and its industry, but also to the entire Southeast.

The Thurlow Dam was finished as the Great Depression began. The people of Tallassee were spared extreme economic hardship during the Depression because the mills never closed, although at times they ran on reduced schedules. Because the mills continued to operate, other business in Tallassee also survived the Depression.

The 1940s brought a proud and prosperous time to Tallassee. During World War II, the mills and the residents of Tallassee worked hard to supply the U.S. armed forces with cotton duck for tents and cots, cotton drills, twine, and rope. For the first six months of 1942, the Tallassee Mills operated seven days a week to meet the emergency demand of the armed services. Without any increase in facilities, the Tallassee Mills increased production by 225 percent and employed 4,500 workers. During this same time period, more than 2,500 men and women from Tallassee served in the armed services. Tallassee's success and dedication were acknowledged when, on April 7, 1943, the Tallassee Mills received the Army-Navy "E" Award, from the U.S. government for excellence and efficiency in the production of war materials. The "E" Award was the highest honor the nation bestowed "upon citizen soldiers of the war production front" during World War II. More than 7,500, people attended the ceremony and celebration. However, Tallasseeans did not rest on their laurels; the mills earned the award again in 1944 and 1945.

In 1944, the Tallassee Mills celebrated the 100th anniversary of the building of the first mill beside the great falls. At the time of the celebration, the mills were 80 times as large as the first operation in 1844. In addition to recognizing the mills' centennial, the Fourth of July celebration rededicated the community's support of the nation's war effort. The Tallassee Mills invited the entire town of Tallassee to a barbecue (for 5,000 people) held at the Ball Park. In addition to good food, the people of Tallassee gathered to enjoy carnival rides, hear speeches, and tell many stories.

Many have had a voice in telling Tallassee's story. The knowledgeable visitor can see the traces of past chapters in a granite monument, an abandoned armory, a bridge that spans the

Tallapoosa River, mills that stand on the river's edge, and a grand hotel. In 2008, the people of Tallassee celebrated the centennial of the town incorporation. Tallassee's story continues, as do the town's changes.

This book's photographs feature many places and people in Tallassee's story. Some, however, have no doubt been inadvertently omitted, and to these we writers offer our humble apology. This book then is dedicated to all those, seen and unseen within these pages, who took part in and held in their hearts Tallassee's story.

One

EARLY DAYS

Tallassee's early days began with the Native American settlements Talisi and Tukabahchi, both in the vicinity of modern Tallassee. In 1844, the antebellum mill complex was built on the west bank of the river. Taken by noted photographer B. D. Bilbrey (1868–1944), this 1899 view of the Tallassee Mills is from the east side of the Tallapoosa River. (Courtesy THPS.)

In 1775, William Bartram, a natural scientist, visited the Creek towns of Talisi and Tukabahchi in the vicinity of the current town of Tallassee. He wrote in *Travels* that he visited "Talasse, a town on the Tallapossa River." In 1776, he revisited the area while trying to find some traders who were "setting off from Tukabatchee for Augusta." (Courtesy AUM Library.)

Henry Popple's map of 1733 was the first large-scale map of North America. This section, *The Southeastern Part of the Present United States*, shows the Creek Indian towns of "Tallafe" (Talisi) and "Tocabatchie" (Tukabahchi) and names the Tallapoosa River "Locushatchee." (Courtesy Bill Goss.)

Col. Benjamin Hawkins, a United States Indian agent for over 30 years, wrote the first description of the Tallassee Falls: "The water of the falls, after tumbling over a bed of rock for half a mile, is forced into two channels. The rock is a light gray, very much divided in square blocks of various sizes for building." (Courtesy AUM Library.)

Different spellings for Talisi and Tukabahchi were common, as in the 1818 *Towns of the Creek Confederacy as Shown on an Early Map of Georgia*. This map also shows the many Creek towns in the area and Talisi's proximity to "Ft. Thoulouse now Ft. Jackson" where the Creeks surrendered. (Courtesy Bill Goss.)

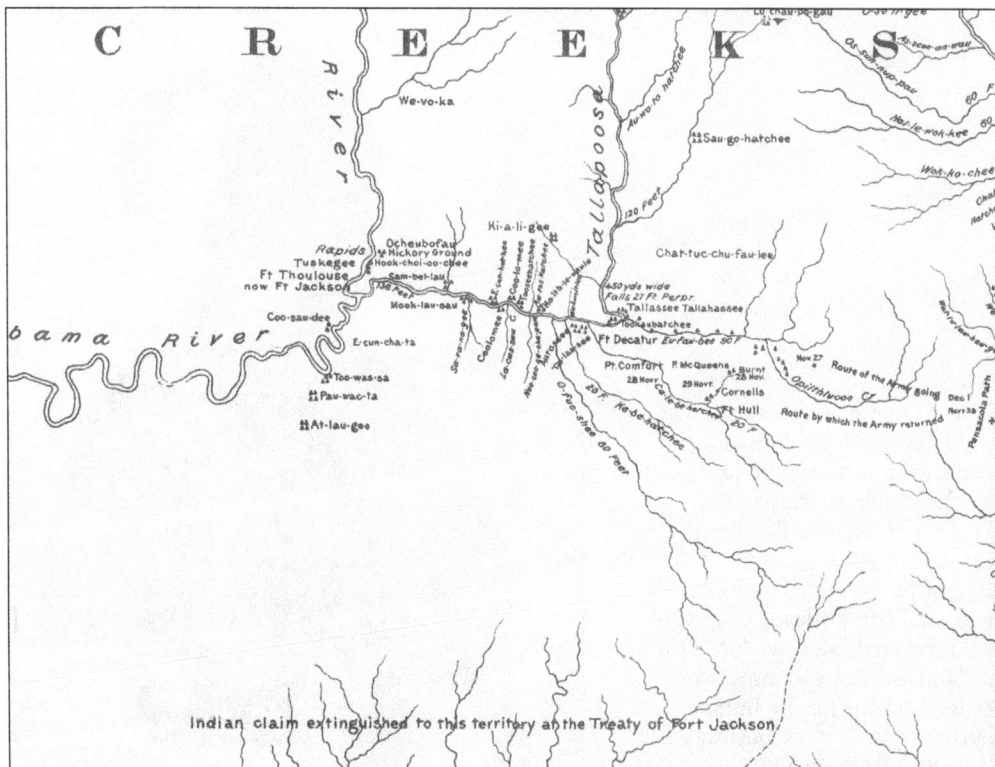

English Baptist missionary Rev. Lee Compere and his wife, Suzanne, arrived at Tukabahchi in 1817. Compere did not convert many Creeks. In 1829, he established the First Baptist Church of Montgomery. Compere's advocacy for the Creeks angered his contemporaries. He wrote, "I have the honor of being despised as a missionary, viewed with contempt as an Indian's friend, and reproached with the unfortunate name of 'Englishman.'" (Courtesy First Baptist Church Montgomery.)

Chief Menawa, a legendary chief of the Upper Creek Indians, was inspired by Tecumseh to lead the Red Sticks at the decisive Battle of Horseshoe Bend in the war against the United States in 1813–1814. Wounded multiple times and left for dead, he survived and recovered. Menawa lost all his land and possessions to white settlers and left for the Indian Territories in 1836. (Courtesy AUM Special Collections.)

Tecumseh visited Tukabahchi in 1811. He urged the Creeks to join his confederacy and reclaim their native land. His speech included the prophecy that upon returning to Detroit, he would stomp his feet and spread his arms to prove his message was divinely supported. The New Madrid earthquakes and the comet of 1811 were interpreted as fulfilling his prophecy, and the Upper Creeks went to war. (Courtesy AUM Library.)

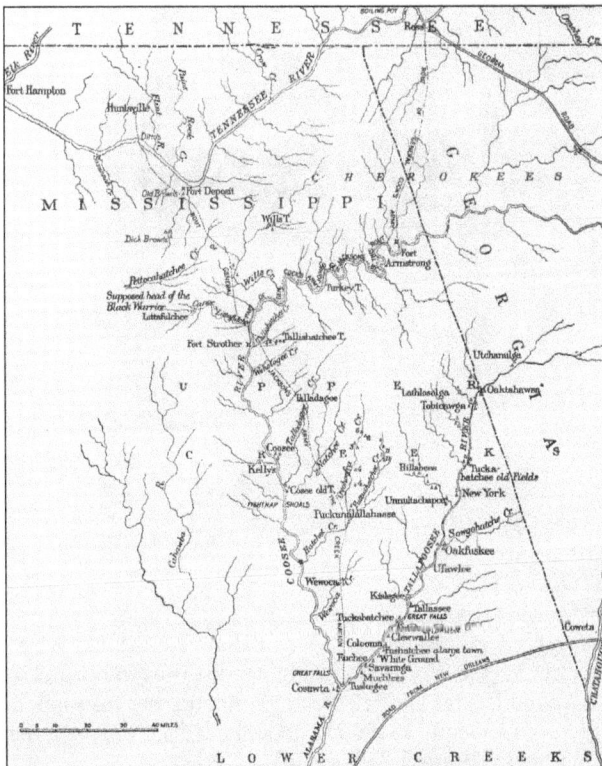

The *Melish Map of 1814 Covering the Seat of War Between the Creek Indians and the Americans in 1813–1814* uses the French spelling of "Tallapoosee" River and designates the older Tukabahchi as "old fields." The two "Great Falls" are Tallassee and the contemporary town of Wetumpka. John Melish settled in America in 1810. He became the first American publisher to specialize in geographical and cartographical works. (Courtesy Bill Goss.)

15

O-POTH-LE-YO-HO-LO.

SPEAKER OF THE COUNCILS.

Nº 34.

RICE, RUTTER & CO. Publishers

Opothleyoholo, born at Tukabahchi, was an Upper Creek leader before and after the relocation to Indian Territory. An advocate of traditional Creek customs, he fought against the Americans in 1813–1814. After the war, regardless of his negotiations with two U.S. presidents and his support for the Second Seminole War, he was forced to relocate. In August 1836, he led a group of about 2,700 Creeks out of Tukabahchi. (Courtesy AUM Special Collections.)

16

PROGRAM

20th Anniversary Meeting
of the

Alabama Anthropological Society
(Organized May 13, 1909)

Commemorating

TUKABAHCHI

The Capital of the Upper Creek Nation
1733

At which time, a Granite Monument upon which is placed a Historical Bronze
Tablet will be unveiled at the Great Council Oak

———

On the old Walter E. Sistrunk Place
near Tallassee

———

Tuesday, May 21st, 1929
4:00 P. M.

In 1929, the Alabama Anthropological Society held a ceremony and raised a monument to mark the site of the Great Council Oak where Tecumseh, Colonel Hawkins, Menawa, Opothleyoholo, and others spoke at Tukabahchi. The area is within Tallassee's city limits. (Courtesy Frederica Dobbs Melton.)

The Tukabahchi Monument exemplifies Tallassee's changes. The bronze plaque, set in a boulder from the Tallapoosa River, was originally placed at Tukabahchi. In 1975, the monument was moved to the Grove, which later became Bicentennial Park. The monument currently stands in front of Tallassee City Hall, which was the old East Tallassee School. (Courtesy Tim Henderson.)

The first mill, the bell tower, and other structures were built on the west side of the Tallapossa River in 1844. This photograph, taken by Charles A. McCluskey as a part of the 1880s collection, *Views of the Tallassee Falls Manufacturing Company*, shows the view of the 1844 mill complex from the east side of the Tallapoosa River. (Courtesy THPS.)

Ambrose Jackson claimed to have lived in Tallassee before the first mill was built in 1844. He worked as a porter for the mill owner, William Barnett. (Courtesy THPS.)

Dam and Saw Mill, from the Canal.

The Tallassee Mills built a sawmill near the dam on the west side bank of the Tallapoosa River. The mills then cut timber for use in building and expanding. This 1880s photograph is from the Charles A. McCluskey collection and is titled *Dam and Saw Mill from the Canal*. (Courtesy THPS.)

Forrest L. McKenzie, the grandson of one of the pioneer planter families of the area, stands on North Ann Street around 1900. The back of Herren Building and the top of the Osceola Hotel are also visible. (Courtesy THPS.)

Forrest L. McKenzie owned three large plantations, three stores in Tallassee and Carrville, and founded the first newspaper in Tallassee. McKenzie is shown here riding his carriage down King Street. The house behind him is one of the Barnett houses, built around 1880; although its appearance is much changed from remodeling, it is still standing. (Courtesy Edward Pattillo.)

In addition to working everyday except Sunday in the mills, many men also worked on farms.

In 1912, an oxen team led by Daniel Herren Sr. (1888–1956) moves a large boiler from the train depot to another location. Taken by noted photographer B. D. Bilbrey, the photograph shows the 1893 Company Store, built by the Tallassee Mills, in the background. (Courtesy THPS.)

Ruth Burton enjoyed riding her horse, Old Dan, around Tallassee and the surrounding countryside. Ruth married James Marvin Herren Sr. (1878–1945) after his wife and her sister, Kate Burton Herren (1879–1929), died. (Courtesy John Andrew Herren.)

Two

A HUB OF THE CONFEDERACY

From 1864 to 1865, the mills and the Confederate armory made Tallassee a hub of the Confederate supply line. The old factory (as the building was called) was renovated and housed the Tallassee Confederate Armory. The mills also produced Confederate uniforms and cloth for tents. Thomas M. Barnett and William M. Marks had constructed the mill that became the armory building of native stone and lumber in 1844. Chartered on December 31, 1841, by the Alabama General Assembly, it was the first textile mill built in Tallassee and the second one built in Alabama. This 1880s photograph is part of the collection by Charles A. McCluskey. (Courtesy THPS.)

Capt. Charles Pattison Bolles, CSA, served as the first commander of the Tallassee Confederate Armory from May 1864 to December 1864. Later he was promoted to the rank of major. (Courtesy AUM Library.)

Robert Harley Jackson (Jack) Mallory (1840–1929), the paternal great-grandfather of Frederica Dobbs Melton, served in the Civil War for the Confederate States of America (CSA) as a private in Company B, 12th Alabama Regiment of the Alabama Infantry from June 17, 1861 until April 10, 1865. (Courtesy Frederica D. Melton.)

View from near the Factory, looking West.

Workers who relocated from Richmond, Virginia, to Tallassee to work in the armory lived with their families in these houses built for mill employees. Living space was scarce, and several families shared the two-room houses. After the Civil War, tradition holds that these residences, still provided for mill employees, were known as Happy Hollow. The 1880s Charles A. McCluskey photograph is titled *View from near the Factory looking West*. (Courtesy THPS.)

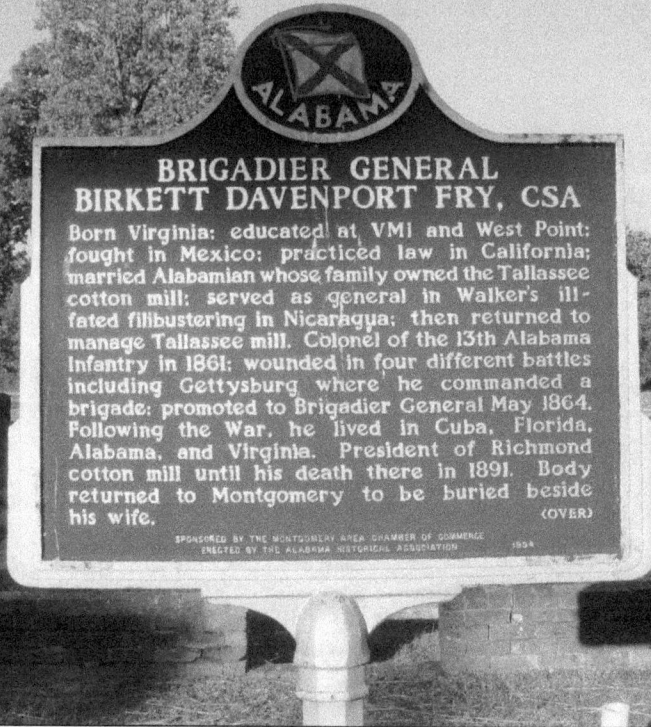

BRIGADIER GENERAL
BIRKETT DAVENPORT FRY, CSA

Born Virginia: educated at VMI and West Point:
fought in Mexico: practiced law in California;
married Alabamian whose family owned the Tallassee
cotton mill: served as general in Walker's ill-
fated filibustering in Nicaragua; then returned to
manage Tallassee mill. Colonel of the 13th Alabama
Infantry in 1861: wounded in four different battles
including Gettysburg where he commanded a
brigade: promoted to Brigadier General May 1864.
Following the War, he lived in Cuba, Florida,
Alabama, and Virginia. President of Richmond
cotton mill until his death there in 1891. Body
returned to Montgomery to be buried beside
his wife.
(OVER)

SPONSORED BY THE MONTGOMERY AREA CHAMBER OF COMMERCE
ERECTED BY THE ALABAMA HISTORICAL ASSOCIATION   1994

Brig. Gen. Birkett Davenport Fry (1822–1891), CSA, served in the 13th Alabama Infantry Regiment, the regiment to which the Tallassee Guards (Company F) was assigned. He was a Confederate officer, a lawyer, and an executive for the Tallassee Manufacturing Company. Fry suggested the Tallassee mills as an armory location to Gen. Josiah Gorgas, who was in charge of Confederate ordnance. (Courtesy Tim Henderson.)

Several houses were built in Tallassee for Confederate officers. These houses may be the only housing the Confederacy built. Three remain in use today. Virginia Scott and Ruth Noble sit on the steps of one of the homes at 301 King Street. The house is used today as an office for the Segrest Law Firm. (Courtesy THPS.)

Residence of B. H. Micou, Prest.

From May 28 to May 30, 1864, CSA officers Lt. Col. James H. Burton and Capt. Charles Pattison Bolles were guests at the home of Benjamin Hall Micou, the owner and president of the mill Barnett, Micou, and Company. During their stay, Burton and Bolles negotiated a contract to use the 1844 mill for a Confederate armory. The Micou house, shown here in 1880, burned in 1909. The house's site today comprises the downtown area. (Courtesy THPS.)

James William Boatwright Sr. worked as a gunsmith at the Tallassee Confederate armory in 1865. The Confederate flag pin on his lapel indicates that he posed for this photograph while attending the 1908 Confederate reunion in Birmingham, Alabama. (Courtesy James H. Boatwright.)

Tallassee's remaining Confederate veterans held a reunion at the old town hall between 1918 and 1925, and posed for this Bilbrey Brothers' photograph. Pictured from left to right are (first row) four unidentified, ? Garrett, Madison Matthew Lambert (with wooden leg), and Robert Harley Jackson (Jack) Mallory; (second row) Jonathan D. Hill, two unidentified, William Marion Benson, unidentified, and James P. (Jim) Kersey; (third row) Berta Coker, holding the Confederate flag. (Courtesy THPS.)

Three

TALLASSEE AND THE TALLAPOOSA

The Tallapoosa River flows through Tallassee. The historic Tallassee Falls on the lower Tallapoosa River have played a significant role in Tallassee's history and industrial development. On the Tallassee Falls in the 1890s, the Tallassee Mills built the gristmill and dam on the west bank of the Tallapoosa River. (Courtesy Bill Goss.)

Falls, from Canal, in rear of Old Factory.

The Tallassee Falls contribute both beauty and prosperity to Tallassee. In the 1880s, Charles A. McCluskey documented the Tallassee Falls, the mills, and the Tallapoosa River with a series of photographs titled *Views of the Tallassee Falls Manufacturing Company*. This scene is from the 1844 Tallassee Mill, on the west bank of the Tallapoosa River and is titled *Falls from Canal in Rear of Old Factory*. (Courtesy THPS.)

View of the Falls, from the Old Factory,

Standing by the 1844 mill, known as the old factory, Charles A. McCluskey captured this view of the falls. Part of his 1880s collection, this view is titled *Views of the Falls from the Old Factory.* (Courtesy THPS.)

Falls of the Tallapoosa, from a rock in mid stream.

In the 1880s, the Tallapoosa River at Tallassee was not yet controlled by modern technology. This photograph, part of the Charles A. McCluskey collection, shows the river's natural flow before the dam and is titled *Falls of Tallapoosa from a Rock in Mid Stream*. (Courtesy THPS.)

The Falls, from Old Factory, at high water.

The Tallapoosa River frequently flooded. Photographed by Charles A. McCluskey in 1880, this view of rushing water is titled *Falls from Old Factory at High Water*. (Courtesy THPS.)

View from the West bank of the River, below the Falls, at high water mark.

The Tallapoosa River, while providing beauty and opportunity, was also a threat at flood stage. In this scene from the lower Tallapoosa River, Charles A. McCluskey shows the river's wild nature in the photograph titled *View from the West Bank of River, Below the Falls, at High Water Mark.* (Courtesy THPS.)

This river scene, taken by Charles A. McCluskey in the 1880s, shows the falls of the Tallapoosa River before the Tallassee Mills dam extended across the entire river. (Courtesy THPS.)

The Tallassee Mills built the 1896 iron trestle bridge to connect east and west Tallassee. This Bilbrey Brothers' photograph is taken from the west side of the lower Tallapoosa River. (Courtesy THPS.)

In 1897, construction began on the Tallassee Mills dam. This view is from the west side looking across the Tallapoosa River. In the Bilbrey Brother's photograph, part of the old dam is in the center, and the coffer dams are on the left. (Courtesy THPS.)

This early suspension cable bridge, constructed by the Tallassee Mills, spanned the lower Tallapoosa River and was used to carry equipment and personnel. Two men are standing on the cable, and one is sitting. Below the cable is a footbridge used to cross the river before the first bridge was built. (Courtesy THPS.)

Flooding was a continual problem in Tallassee's early days. This early Tallassee Mills dam was demolished during a flood of the Tallapoosa River. (Courtesy Bill Goss.)

This scene shows the mill dam at flood stage, looking east to west from Tallapoosa to Elmore County. The Tallassee Mills bridge is in the left foreground. (Courtesy THPS.)

On December 10, 1919, the Tallapoosa River reached flood stage and demolished the upper Tallassee dam of the Montgomery Light and Power Company, the Tallassee Mills dam, and the 1896 iron trestle bridge. The railroad tracks of the Birmingham and Southeastern Railroad and the Tallassee Mills weaving shed on the west side were heavily damaged. (Courtesy Frederica D. Melton.)

During the flood of 1919, the 1896 Tallassee Mills iron trestle bridge was destroyed. A ferry was used until a new bridge could be built. In this 1921 photograph, workers prepare the site for the ferry crossing. (Courtesy Frederica D. Melton.)

After the flood of 1919, the Tallassee Mills erected this temporary bridge on the lower Tallapoosa River at Tallassee to connect the two textiles mills and mill villages. (Courtesy THPS.)

Just two years later, another flood caused extensive damage. In this 1921 photograph, some Tallassee men survey the damage caused by the flood. Some of the railroad tracks, at the left, were washed away. In the background is the Tallassee depot. (Courtesy Frederica D. Melton.)

In 1923, the Tallassee Mills and the Alabama Power Company reached an agreement for the joint use of the power generated at Tallassee. It is believed that this photograph shows some of the construction and improvements at the Tallassee Mills power plant in 1923. (Courtesy THPS.)

In the 1930s, as now, when flood gates are open, the Tallapoosa River rushes over the dam. This view includes both the Thurlow Dam and the powerhouse at Tallassee. (Courtesy Bill Goss.)

Tallapoosa River, Tallassee Falls, Tallassee, Ala., "The Niagara of the South"

Thurlow Dam, built in c. 1928 by the Alabama Power Company at Tallassee, is shown during flood stage, in this 1940s photograph. The water pouring over the dam was known as the "Niagara of the South." (Courtesy Bill Goss.)

A colorful parade depicting Tallassee's history preceded the dedication of Tallassee's Benjamin Fitzpatrick Bridge on December 10, 1940. Riding on the Alabama Power Company float, from left to right, three ladies symbolically represent the major dams: Kathleen Wade (Upper Tallassee, now Yates), Rachel Daniel (Thurlow Dam), and Joyce Hawkins (Martin Dam). (Courtesy THPS.)

This float, still receiving finishing touches, represented Tallassee's early beginnings as a Native American settlement. (Courtesy THPS.)

On December 10, 1940, Tallassee's Benjamin Fitzpatrick Bridge was formally opened and dedicated. More than 6,000 people attended the ceremony and walked across the bridge from the east side (Tallapoosa County) to the west side (Elmore County). At the time, the bridge was one of the most unusual in the world, and it continues to link East and West Tallassee. (Courtesy THPS.)

46

Four

A TEXTILE TOWN

Until recently, Tallassee has been a textile town. For 161 years, the Tallassee Mills operated in Tallassee, producing cotton and woolen textiles. The first textile mill in Tallassee was chartered by the General Assembly of Alabama on December 31, 1841, and was run by water power from the Tallapoosa River. By 1870, the Tallassee Mills were the largest textile mills in Alabama. In the foreground of this photograph, on the left, is the 1897 mill, known as Mill No. 2, on the east bank of the Tallapoosa River; in the center is the 1897 bridge; and at the top center is the antebellum mill complex on the west side. (Courtesy Bill Goss.)

Standing in front of a Case thrasher in the 1890s at the side of "White Store" are, from left to right, James William Dobbs (1866–1947); unidentified; Dobb's son, Fred Dobbs (seated); and unidentified. On top of the Case thrasher is Fred Dobb's son, Euell Dobbs, and unidentified. (Courtesy Frederica D. Melton.)

The Tallassee Mills powerhouses, one on each side of the Tallapoosa River, contained the waterwheels that operated the early mills. Power from the wheels was transmitted by belts and shafts to the machines. Shown in this 1920s photograph of the powerhouse in East Tallassee are, from left to right, unidentified, Micajah L. (Cage) Anthony (1873–1936), and unidentified. (Courtesy Reginald Anthony.)

48

In July 1916, a tornado hit Tallassee and damaged many houses in the mill village on the west side of the Tallapoosa River. This photograph shows the destruction on South Ann Street near the downtown area. (Courtesy THPS.)

A Tallassee Mills worker's house on James Street and part of the Company Store were damaged by the 1916 tornado in Tallassee. (Courtesy THPS.)

Men from the Tallassee Mills work in one of the gullies on South Ann Street. (Courtesy THPS.)

On Wednesday, September 29, 1920, the overseers (supervisors) of the Shawmut Mill in Shawmut, Alabama, came to Tallassee and were guests of the management and overseers of the Tallassee Mills. The visitors toured the town of Tallassee and the Tallassee Mills and were served a chicken dinner at the club house in East Tallassee (currently the library). (Courtesy THPS.)

Pictured from left to right are three section supervisors working in the spinning department of Tallassee Mills No. 2 in East Tallassee: Alva McClellan, Jesse Yates, and John Miller. (Courtesy THPS.)

The image, first published in the *Briefs*, a news booklet the mills printed monthly, shows several men, the spinning room overhaulers. They are identified, from left to right, as J. H. Hagood, Howard Taylor, Bob Yates, and Luther Lambert. (Courtesy THPS.)

The 1897 mill was in East Tallassee. The photograph is of the south side of the mill and was taken prior to 1923, when Mill No. 3 was built on this site. (Courtesy THPS.)

Founded in 1925, the Tallassee Community Hospital was a part of the Tallassee Mills. Shown in this 1930s photograph is the second community hospital in East Tallassee, which served the community from 1937 to 1975. In 1975, the Community Hospital, a nonprofit, community-owned-and-operated acute care facility, relocated to 805 Friendship Road. (Courtesy THPS.)

J. F. Mann, a clerk, stands in Tallassee's first variety store in 1920. Joyce Bryan owned the store. (Courtesy THPS.)

Dobbs' Mercantile Store in Jordanville, a part of Tallassee, sold groceries, fresh produce, meat, and Jazz Feeds. Pictured in this 1919 photograph are, from left to right, Harley Dobbs, unidentified, and Fred Dobbs. (Courtesy Frederica D. Melton.)

The *Mount Vernon–Woodberry News* was published monthly in the 1920s by the Mount Vernon–Woodberry Mills, Inc., of Baltimore, Maryland, the owner of the Tallassee Mills. The publication contained news and pictures from all of the textile mills in the corporation. The Tallassee Mills were always well represented. (Courtesy THPS.)

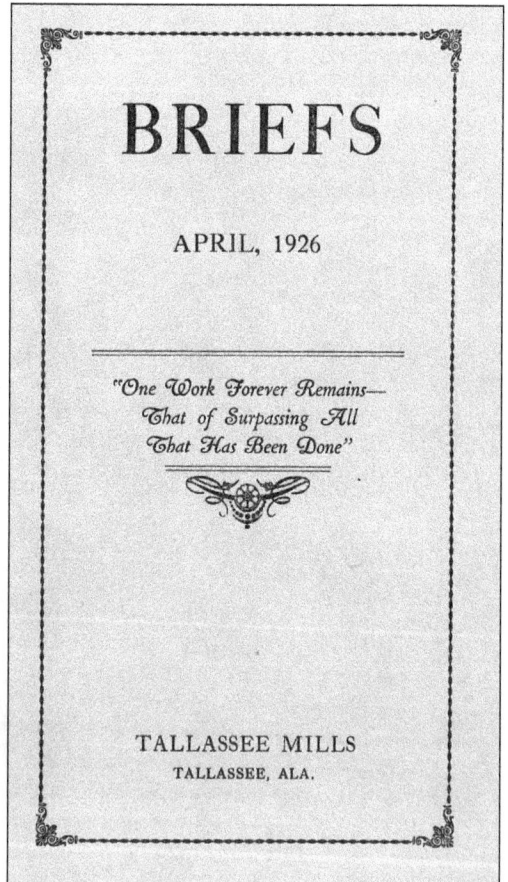

The Tallassee Mills *Briefs*, a news booklet published by the Tallassee Mills from 1917 to 1932, contained news, features, and pictures about Tallassee, the management, and the employees of the mills. It was published monthly, and copies were distributed to every employee. (Courtesy THPS.)

The old wooden Tallassee Mills Company Store in East Tallassee, which burned in 1923, was replaced by this large brick one in 1926. The new building contained a dry goods store, a grocery store, a drugstore, the East Tallassee post office, a cafe, a furniture store, and an upstairs room for the Masonic lodge. (Courtesy Pete Cottle.)

This 1930s view of the 1893 Tallassee Mills Company Store in West Tallassee shows the renovated store with its 1927 brick facade face-lift and two additional wings—the drugstore (left) and the post office (right). (Courtesy Pete Cottle.)

The Tallassee Mills built two mill villages for its workers, one in West Tallassee and the other in East Tallassee. These houses, located in the first block of Redden Avenue in East Tallassee, were built in 1925. (Courtesy THPS.)

Built in the 1930s, this duplex stands opposite the East Tallassee Baptist Church, on Central Boulevard. (Courtesy THPS.)

This oak tree stood on the west side of Redden Avenue in East Tallassee for many years. In 1930, Howard Hall, the son of Charles Hall, decided to become a "sitter," in his tree house. He began his sitting at 10:00 a.m. on July 29, 1930, and did not come down again until August 25, 1930. (Courtesy THPS.)

Bales of cotton were stored on the loading dock of Mill No. 2 in East Tallassee. For many years, the Tallassee Mills operated its own cotton gin. Local farmers brought their cotton to the Tallassee Mills for ginning. The Tallassee Mills cotton gin produced from 1,500 to 2,000 bales of cotton a season. (Courtesy THPS.)

On Saturday afternoons, the merchants in Tallassee gave cash and merchandise to entice shoppers to the downtown stores. This 1928 Bilbrey Studio photograph was taken in front of the Woodall Hotel (now Hotel Talisi) on Sistrunk Street. (Courtesy THPS.)

This 1930s aerial view of Tallassee shows Lake Talisi, the Thurlow Dam and powerhouse, the Tallapoosa River, the antebellum textile mills (lower part of photograph), the 1920 mill bridge, the 1897 and 1924 textile mills on the east side (upper part of photograph), and the east side elementary school, hospital, community library, and mill village. (Courtesy Bill Goss.)

The site, on the corner of North Ann Street and Barnett Boulevard where the present Tallassee Police Department is located, is another example of Tallassee's many changes. The first building erected there was the Tallassee Mills Company Store, c. 1844, which was called the "White Store" because it was painted white. It burned around 1896 and a second Company Store, a stone two-story building, replaced it; however, it also burned a few years later. The third building on this site was the town community hall, built about 1905 and shown in this 1930s photograph. The town community hall also housed the West Mount Vernon Movie Theatre. (Courtesy Pete Cottle.)

The Woodall Hotel (now the Hotel Talisi) opened in 1928 in downtown Tallassee and has operated continuously for 80 years. Under the leadership of only four owners, it has become an east-central Alabama and west-central Georgia dining tradition. Here on a busy Saturday afternoon in 1928, the marquee for the Palace Café, the hotel's restaurant, is seen above the crowd. (Courtesy THPS.)

Five

FUN TIMES

Although Tallasseeans worked hard, they made time for fun. The Tallassee Mills Milstead Band, organized by Andrew Jackson Milstead (the superintendent of the Tallassee Mills from 1876 to 1912), and the Tallassee Mummers in their fantastic disguises pose at one of their festive events in the 1890s. (Courtesy THPS.)

Three mummers in their costumes get ready for a performance in the 1920s. (Courtesy THPS.)

Two gentlemen cruise by McKenzie's store in a c. 1913 automobile. (Courtesy THPS.)

Pictured from left to right, Marjorie and Forest Ballentine, children of Lonnie Ballentine, have fun pretending to drive in a toy car. (Courtesy THPS.)

Pictured from left to right, Julian Richardson, age 4, and his brother Robert Richardson, age 8, sons of R. W. Richardson, play with their pet calf. (Courtesy THPS.)

Tallasseeans Donna Ruth Burton (who later married Marvin Herren Sr.) and her friend Joe Abney sit on Scott's Bridge below Tiller's Crossroads in Tallapoosa County. (Courtesy John Andrew Herren.)

Weekend dances were popular occasions. In this *c.* 1912 photograph, some Red Hill and Tallassee musicians pose. Pictured from left to right are (first row) Bertie Carl Dopson, banjo, and Alvin Berry Dopson, fiddle; (second row) Aubrey Melton; Elmer Dopson, banjo; John Castleberry; and Lester Melton. (Courtesy Paula Eller Castleberry.)

The Goss brothers' band was popular in the 1920s and 1930s at dances and other events in the Tallassee area and Panama City, Florida. Pictured in this early 1920s Bilbrey Studio photograph are, from left to right, Grady Coleman, Lemuel Goss, and Frank Goss. Missing from the picture are Johnny Goss and Thomas Goss, who were also members of the band. (Courtesy Betty Blakely Mason.)

Ready to sing a song are, from left to right, Lizzie Baker, Ozella Baker (with guitar), and Minnie Baker. (Courtesy Jane Baker Bryant.)

First published in the June 1925 Tallassee Mills *Briefs*, the caption for this photograph reads "Otis Taunton on his way to church." (Courtesy THPS.)

Willie Reeves plays his banjo in this 1920s photograph. (Courtesy THPS.)

Lorenna Gauntt, daughter of C. R. Gauntt, and two friends from Georgia find a way to cool off on a hot summer day. (Courtesy THPS.)

Four Tallasseeans pose in this c. 1912 automobile in front of a painted background. Pictured from left to right are Dr. William Smith, unidentified, James Benolian Baker (paternal grandfather of Jane Baker Bryant), and unidentified. (Courtesy Jane Baker Bryant.)

Dr. William A. Warren owned this c. 1905 Reo Runabout, the first automobile in Tallassee. Dr. Warren was a physician who lived in Carrville, Alabama. In the driver's seat is Dovard Roye, who drove the car for Dr. Warren. The early Reo Motor Car Company of Lansing, Michigan, was named after the initials of automobile pioneer–inventor Ransom E. Olds, who also gave his name to the Oldsmobile. (Courtesy THPS.)

Sports were popular activities. The mills, the company stores, and both East and West Tallassee sponsored ball teams for every season. Here an East Tallassee baseball team poses in front of their equipment. (Courtesy THPS.)

In this *c.* 1915 photograph, the members of the Tallassee Mills Company Store baseball team are, from left to right, two unidentified, Dave Golden, Wesley Gaither, unidentified, ? Golden, unidentified, Tim Golden, James B. Baker, and John Golden. (Courtesy Jane Baker Bryant.)

The *c.* 1921 Tallassee Mills baseball team includes, from left to right, (first row) Tom Mason, outfield; Bill Dobbs, outfield; Bubba Totty, pitcher; Tim Golden, catcher; and Jack Noble, second base; (second row) Carvel Woodall, outfield; Fred Dobbs, catcher; Aubie Howard, shortstop; John Golden, first base; and Forrest Fincher, utility; (third row) Robert Cottle, scorekeeper; Bill Turrentine, bookie; Jim Hornsby Sr., team manager; and Ed Harris, Tallassee Mills agent and team promoter. (Courtesy Frederica D. Melton.)

Pictured from left to right are members of the *c.* 1921 Tallassee Mills baseball team: (first row) Bill Dobbs, Tim Golden, Bubba Totty, and Aubie Howard; (second row) B. B. Comer, Charlie Martin, Forrest Fincher, Tom Mason, John Golden, Jack Noble, Fred Dobbs, Robert Cottle, unidentified, and Jim Hornsby Sr. (Courtesy Frederica D. Melton.)

The Tallassee Mills sponsored the first Fourth of July picnic at the ballpark in 1912. The event became an annual tradition and continued until the 1950s. The biggest activity of the year, it attracted nearly 6,000 people. Various events, contests, and carnival rides provided entertainment. Large barrels of lemonade were everywhere, barbecue was served, and dinner was spread on the ground. A baseball game closed the festivities. In this 1940s photograph, volunteers get the serving lines for barbecue ready. (Courtesy THPS.)

Six

DRESSED UP

The people of Tallassee enjoyed getting dressed up. In the 1920s, the Daniel Herren family and friends went to Stone Creek in East Tallassee to picnic and to relax in the cool shade by the water. (Courtesy John Andrew Herren.)

Three unidentified Tallassee ladies are dressed in their Sunday finery for their Bilbrey Studio portrait. (Courtesy THPS.)

Two friends, Lottie Hethcox (left) and Irene Gray, wear fashionable sailor suits in this Bilbrey Studio photograph. (Courtesy John Andrew Herren.)

In 1917, the James Benolian Baker family pose for this Bilbrey Studio family portrait photograph. Pictured from left to right are Addie Bridgman Baker, Wilson Baker, and James B. Baker. (Courtesy Jane Baker Bryant.)

Wilson Baker (all grown up from previous photograph) and Obie Bridgman (right) pose for this 1920s Bilbrey Studio photograph. (Courtesy Jane Baker Bryant.)

Standing proudly on his own in a sailor suit, Raymond Lee Kinsaul is 22 months old. (Courtesy THPS.)

The Tallassee chapter of the American Red Cross was first organized during World War I. Since 1918, it has been an important part of the Tallassee community. It is believed that these ladies are members of the Tallassee chapter of the American Red Cross during World War I. (Courtesy THPS.)

Wiley and Minnie Baker Powell pose for their portrait at Bilbrey Studio. (Courtesy Jane Baker Bryant.)

Frank and Clara Mae Hepburn posed for this Bilbrey Studio photograph, first published in the *Briefs* in February 1927, shortly after their marriage in December 1926. (Courtesy THPS.)

This c. 1914 photograph shows, from left to right, Ella McClendon, Ruth Burton Herren, and ? Bledsoe wearing fancy hats in Lanett, Alabama. (Courtesy John Andrew Herren.)

Sitting on a log and dressed up is Wallace Reid Melton, the oldest son of Lester V. Melton and Myrtle Davis Melton. He is also the brother of Davis and Miller Melton. (Courtesy THPS.)

Lizzie Baker (left) and Minnie Baker are shown in this undated Bilbrey Studio photograph. (Courtesy Jane Baker Bryant.)

Velma Causey (left) and Gladys McCain, friends and coworkers in the Tallassee Mills, are dressed up and ready to go. (Courtesy THPS.)

Pictured here in this Bilbrey Studio photograph are Ralph Hill (left) and Elizabeth Hill, the grandchildren of R. P. Betts. (Courtesy THPS.)

Mary Stough (left) and Georgie Ingram are wearing identical coats c. 1920. (Courtesy Ella Castleberry.)

Even babies dressed up for their Bilbrey Studio photographs. Murray Woodrow Duke is shown in this 1900s photograph. (Courtesy THPS.)

Lurline Duett, the daughter of B. J. Duett, poses in a fashionable, fur-trimmed dress. (Courtesy THPS.)

This 1930 photograph shows Stowe Hill when he was 16. (Courtesy THPS.)

Taken in the 1930s, it is believed that this photograph is of Ola Lee Crepps, who married Francis M. (Frank) Guy. (Courtesy THPS.)

In this *c.* 1897 Bilbrey Studio photograph, James B. Baker (1892–1962) stands for his formal portrait. (Courtesy Jane Baker Bryant.)

This *c.* 1916 photograph shows, from left to right, Loraine Segrest, Joe Burton, and Ruth Burton. (Courtesy John Andrew Herren.)

Dressed in their Sunday best, an unidentified family sits on the running board of their car in the early 1900s. (Courtesy THPS.)

Pictured from left to right are Charles Clark, Edward Sides, and Obie Sides. (Courtesy THPS.)

Wilson Baker and his dog Snowball pose for this *c.* 1921 photograph. (Courtesy Jane Baker Bryant.)

Shown here is a young Charles Wesley Lambert, dressed up and ready to go to war. (Courtesy THPS.)

Showing off her pretty dress is the granddaughter of Sam and Estell Webster. (Courtesy THPS.)

Seven

FAMILIES AND FRIENDS

Family and friends were an important part of life in Tallassee. George Washington Bridgman, his wife, Nancy Ella Woodall Bridgman, and 10 of their 11 children are pictured at their home in Tallassee in this c. 1902 Bilbrey Studio photograph. Shown from left to right are (first row) Nancy Woodall Bridgman, George W. Bridgman, Willie Carlton Bridgman, and John Harvey Bridgman; (second row) Addie Bridgman, Henrietta Bridgman, Lela Bridgman, Albert Bridgman, David Bridgman, William Bridgman, Jesse Bridgman, and Obediah Bridgman. (Courtesy Jane Baker Bryant.)

Mary Louise Sellers, a daughter of W. G. Sellers, poses with the family dog c. 1921. (Courtesy THPS.)

Shown here are Johnny Rowe (left) and his son, Johnny Rowe Jr., with his pipe. (Courtesy THPS.)

James B. Baker; his wife, Addie Bridgman Baker; his son, Wilson Baker; and the family dog are shown in this early 1920s photograph. (Courtesy Jane Baker Bryant.)

The descendants of John Calvin Jordan are shown in this 1899 photograph. Pictured from left to right are (first row) John Landers, Bink Landers, Byron Melton, Herbert Jordan, and Fairy Jordan; (second row) Idilla Jordan Spivey, Curtis Spivey (in her lap), Alfonza Jordan, John Thomas Melton, Aldridge Melton (in his lap), Amanda Pevy Jordan, John C. Jordan, Leonar Jordan Tucker, and Will Tucker; (third row) Love Landers, Corrie Jordan Melton, Viola Jordan, and Anna Jordan. The log cabin was built by John Calvin Jordan about 1865 when he returned from the Civil War. It is still in use today in the Red Hill community. (Courtesy Peggy Stanfield Landers.)

These Tallassee scouts pose in front of the Club House (currently the library). The Club House

From the early 1920s until the 1970s, the Tallassee Mills and the Tallassee City Board of Education supported both Girl and Boy Scouts. In this 1920s photograph, Tallassee Boy Scout Troop No. 8 demonstrates scouting skills at the scout hut on the campus of the Tallassee High School. (Courtesy Tallassee City Board of Education.)

served as a community center for East Tallassee. (Courtesy THPS.)

Homer Alexander (left) and Merlyn Drake, friends and coworkers at the Tallassee Mills, pose for this photograph that was printed in the *Briefs*. (Courtesy THPS.)

Malcolm Camp (left), age 11, and his sister Vennie Camp, age 9, were the children of S. M. Camp of Benson Avenue in East Tallassee. (Courtesy THPS.)

Members of the Dopson, Landers, and Mask families and friends are shown in front of the old Dopson home in the Red Hill community near Tallassee. Pictured from left to right are (first row) Maude Shores, John Castleberry, James Castleberry, John Strength, Alvin Dopson (fiddle), and Bertie Dopson (banjo); (second row) Charlie Mask, Love Landers, John Landers, Josephine Mask, Eula Taylor, Maude Ingram, Carrie Mask, Nora Mask, and Elmer Dopson (banjo); (third row) Lester Melton, Robert Mask, Aubrey Melton, Bink Landers, and three unidentified; (fourth row) William Griffith, Hermon Griffith, Ollie Griffith, Irene Mask, Will Dopson, Georgie Dopson, and unidentified. (Courtesy Paula Eller Castleberry.)

First published in the *Briefs*, this photograph
shows Lucy Wilkerson and her chickens.
(Courtesy THPS.)

This photograph shows Alice Hamby
Lacy on a brisk autumn day in Tallassee.
(Courtesy THPS.)

Blanchard Milstead (Mick) Crockett plays with his dog Paul. (Courtesy Jane Baker Bryant.)

Shown here are Ralph Bence and his dog. (Courtesy THPS.)

Marion Hutchens and Sarah Hilyer pose with their grandparents in this 1930s photograph. Shown from left to right are Sarah Hilyer, granddaughter; William A. Hilyer (seated); Marion Hutchens, grandson; and Ann Varner Hilyer. (Courtesy Dale Hilyer Dozier.)

This c. 1934 photograph shows the family of Ezekiel Jones Crockett gathered at the home of Thomas David Crockett in south Tallassee. Standing in front of the house are, from left to right, Thomas D. Crockett, Madison A. Crockett, Alberta Elizabeth Crockett, Mattie Lilly Crockett, Blanchard M. Crockett, Ezekiel J. Crockett (who lived to age 103), Ezekiel's wife Frances Altha Crockett (who died in 1935), Duncan E. Crockett, Eula Louise Crockett, Oscar R. Crockett, Robert H. Crockett, and Clarence G. Crockett. (Courtesy Jane Baker Bryant.)

The Tallassee Mills maintained a guest house for the convenience of its visitors. In this mid-1940s photograph, James E. Harris (left), vice president of Mount Vernon–Woodberry Mills, and an unidentified lady sit on the back porch of the Tallassee Mills guest house. (Courtesy THPS.)

James William Boatwright Sr., the machinist who worked at the Confederate armory, married and had a large family. His sons, who also lived in Tallassee or in communities close by, are, from left to right, Daniel Webster, Henry Clay, Jefferson Davis, James William Jr., and George Washington. (Courtesy James H. Boatwright.)

Pictured in this *c.* 1930 photograph are the descendants of Charles J. Cottle (1869–1916). Shown from left to right are (first row) Willa Carroll Cottle, William Archie Cottle, Lois E. Cottle, Robert L. Cottle, Sarah Carlisle Cottle, Charles A. Cottle, and William W. Cottle; (second row) Charles Brooks, Jacqueline Cottle, Eloise Cottle, Minna Virginia Cottle, and Margaret Cottle; (third row) Louise Cottle, Annie Katherine Cottle Brooks, Harold B. Cottle Sr., Mildred Elizabeth Cottle, Minna (Cot) Harris (the wife of Charles J. Cottle), Minna's brother James Harris, Betty Harris Crockett, and Will Crockett. (Courtesy Pete Cottle.)

Built in 1855, Herren Hill is a historic antebellum home in Tallassee. Shown in front of Herren Hill, the family home, are, from left to right, Frances Flournoy Herren, her husband Arnold Whitfield Herren Jr., and their daughter Alice Herren. (Courtesy Herren family.)

Family and friends have always been proud of the men and women from Tallassee who serve in the armed forces. Pictured here in April 1918 in Germany are members of Company D, 113th Supply Train, 38th Division, U.S. Army of the American Expeditionary Forces (AEF) during World War I. A Tallasseean, Fred Dobbs, is the first person from the left in the third row. He served in Germany from April 9, 1918, until July 9, 1919. (Courtesy Frederica D. Melton.)

Eight

THE THREE RS

Early educators taught the three Rs—reading, 'riting, and 'rithmatic. Schools were not publicly supported in Alabama until the early 1900s. The present Tallassee school system began after 1915. Before then, Tallassee used several buildings as schools: the Lodge Hall on the corner of James and Ann Streets; the old "White Store" from 1893 to 1897, a building on Dubois Street between Barnett and King Streets; the building on the corner of Barnett and Marks (later changed to Preer) Streets; and after 1898, the old Methodist church building, which had been moved from King Street over to Barnett Street. In 1916, a new school was built in Tallassee and contained grades one through twelve. In 1928, the 1916 Tallassee School burned. It was replaced by the 1929 Tallassee High School, containing grades one through twelve. Pictured here is the 1916 Tallassee School and its students. (Courtesy Tallassee City Board of Education.)

Students at Miss Clara Barnett's School in Tallassee pose in front of the schoolhouse. The school was located in the vicinity of where the Tallassee Quick Freeze was later built in Jordanville. (Courtesy Edward Pattillo.)

This c. 1922 photograph shows one of the early Tallassee schools. Only three of these individuals can be identified. On the first row from the left, the ninth student is Wilson Baker; on the second row, the teacher is ? Denton and the seventh student is Roy Taylor. (Courtesy Jane Baker Bryant.)

Pictured here is one of the early Tallassee schools. The school and the individuals are unidentified. (Courtesy THPS.)

Pictured here in this Bilbrey Studio photograph, taken in front of the Bilbrey Jewelry Store, is the 1921 Tallassee High School football team. Shown from left to right are (first row) Edgar Hoyle, substitute; Willie Langley, right tackle; Henry Homer, right end; Jim Hurston, right guard; Morrell Horn, center; Dan Mason, left guard; Jack Wright, left tackle; and Louis Taunton, substitute; (second row) Morland Hornsby, quarterback; Jake Catchings, halfback; Tom Mason, fullback; and Austin Buce, halfback. (Courtesy THPS.)

Before 1919, the East and West Tallassee schools were separate. In that year, they were combined under one superintendent. Pictured here is the 1925 East Tallassee School, which now serves as the Tallassee City Hall. (Courtesy THPS.)

Pictured here in this Bilbrey Studio photograph is the 1926 Tallassee High School basketball team in front of the 1916 Tallassee School. (Courtesy Tallassee City Board of Education.)

The 1927 Tallassee High School football team, in practice uniforms, is shown at the ballpark. (Courtesy Tallassee City Board of Education.)

The 1916 school burned on November 11, 1928. This 1929 photograph, taken at the rear of Tallassee High School, shows the new school under construction. The ashes in the foreground at the site where the Stumberg Gymnasium now sits are from the 1916 school. (Courtesy Tallassee City Board of Education.)

Luette Kilpatrick, a teacher from Shady Grove, Alabama, sits at the entrance to the 1916 Tallassee School. She taught the second grade at the Tallassee Elementary School from 1925 to 1927 and was one of the favorite teachers. (Courtesy Reginald Anthony.)

On November 13, 1929, the new Tallassee High School building, shown here, was ready for occupancy. An evening program to celebrate the completion of the school was held; Dr. A. F. Harman, Alabama superintendent of education, was present. On November 14–15, 1929, an open house was held for students, parents, and the community. (Courtesy Tallassee City Board of Education.)

Pictured here is one of the 1929 first-grade classes at Tallassee Elementary School. The teacher, shown at the back, is Mildred Gillis. (Courtesy Tallassee City Board of Education.)

Pictured here in 1929 are 45 pupils of an elementary class at Tallassee Elementary School. (Courtesy Tallassee City Board of Education.)

This 1929 photograph shows the library and study hall room in the new 1929 Tallassee High School. The stack room, containing the reference and library books, was in an adjoining room. (Courtesy Tallassee City Board of Education.)

In 1929, the industrial arts classes were part of the curriculum at Tallassee High School. Shown here are six unidentified members of the shop class with tables they constructed. (Courtesy Tallassee City Board of Education.)

Shown here in this 1929 picture is the industrial arts (general shop) class at Tallassee High School with teacher F. H. DuBose (on the right). (Courtesy Tallassee City Board of Education.)

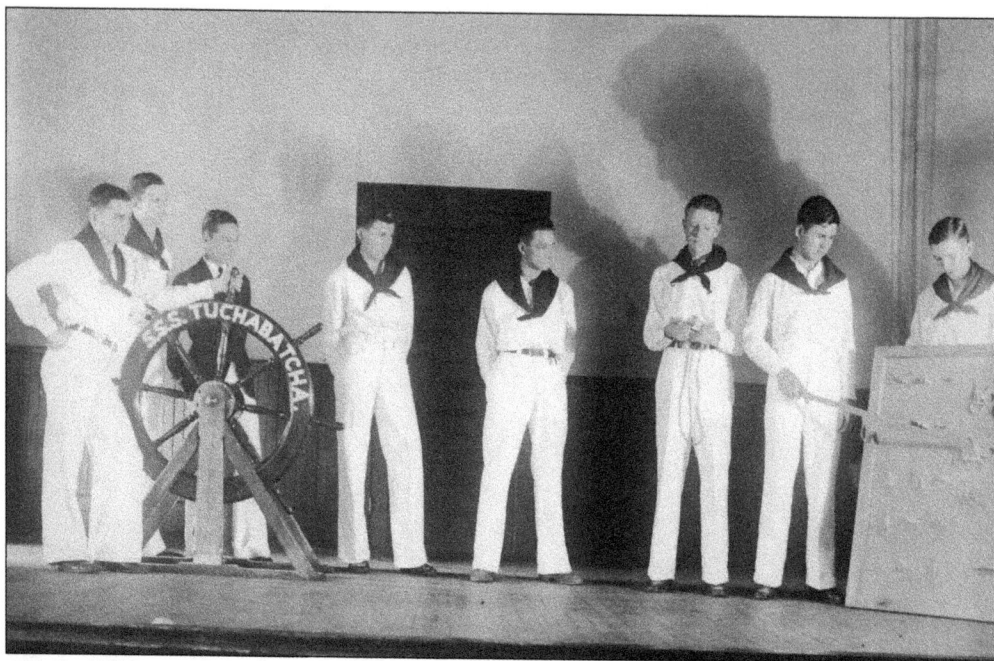

As part of the new curriculum at Tallassee High School in the late 1920s, 1930s, and 1940s, assembly programs were conducted by clubs, classes, and members of the community on Monday, Wednesday, and Friday for the student body. Here a group of senior scouts demonstrate their skills in knot tying. (Courtesy Tallassee City Board of Education.)

In an assembly program, members of the physics class at Tallassee High School demonstrate the power of energy, motion, and force. (Courtesy Tallassee City Board of Education.)

This 1929 Tallassee Elementary School class culminates its study of the Creek (Muskogee) Indians who lived in the Tallassee area by dressing like the Native Americans. (Courtesy Tallassee City Board of Education.)

Pictured here in 1929 in the Tallassee High School auditorium is one of the elementary classes presenting a Christmas program for the students in grades one through six. (Courtesy Tallassee City Board of Education.)

This 1929 photograph depicts a scene from a play performed by students at Tallassee High School. (Courtesy Tallassee City Board of Education.)

Pictured here is a scene from a 1930 assembly program performed by the students in Gladys McNair's class and presented in the new high school auditorium. (Courtesy Tallassee City Board of Education.)

Unidentified members of the 1931–1932 Red Hill School in the Red Hill community are pictured. (Courtesy Paula Eller Castleberry.)

Girls and boys made up the 1930 Red Hills School basketball team. Pictured from left to right are (first row) Tennyson Dopson (teacher), Kirmet Griffith, Ida Fay Dopson, Clayton Thornton, two unidentified, and Lamar McDonald; (second row) Hazel Faircloth (teacher), Helen Graham, Horace Ingram, Nell Nelson, Cullen Warren, and two unidentified. (Courtesy Paula Eller Castleberry.)

Shown here is the 1930 Tallassee High School basketball team in front of the new 1929 Tallassee High School. All of the players are unidentified. (Courtesy Tallassee City Board of Education.)

The 1931 Tallassee High School football team, coached by A. E. Choate (standing on the right), is shown in this Bilbrey Studio photograph. Pictured from left to right are (first row) Ray Lett, Lanier Roton, Orville Blake, and Bennie Little; (second row) Kenzie McInnish, Linwood Gresham, Lewis Holley, Upton Higgins, Ben Wilbanks, Pete Plant, and Parker James; (third row) Sellers Holloway (manager), Jack Golden, Charles Bowen, Bryant Manning, Herman Caldwell, Virgil Redden, Hershall Howard, and Leon Melton; (fourth row) unidentified, Marvin Meadows, unidentified, Wood Billingsley, Robert Lackey, and Sam Baker; (fifth row) Skinner Vardaman, Jones Harris, unidentified, Tom Bowen, Howard Golden, and unidentified; (sixth row) unidentified, Howard Mullins, Neil Richardson, two unidentified, Douglas Baker, Ralph Burton, and John Thompson. (Courtesy Bennie Little.)

Photographed at the west side of Tallassee High School is the 1933 football team. Pictured from left to right are (first row) Ralph Burton, Calvin Warren, Marvin Meadows, Louis Holley, Bennie Little, Wilson Jolley, Durwood Melton, and Orville Blake; (second row) Howard Golden, Tom Bowen, Jack Golden, and Herman Caldwell. In the left background is the West Tallassee teacherage. (Courtesy Bennie Little.)

Pictured in front of the East Tallassee School is its faculty in the late 1930s. Shown from left to right are (first row) Audrey Holloway, unidentified, ? Bell, Pearl Smith, and Ellen Martin; (second row) Henry Parrish (principal), Ruth Coker, Tommie Ransom, Jewel Blocker, Mamie Tomlin, Minnie Cofield, Julia Duffy, and unidentified. (Courtesy Vera Frances Cullars.)

For many years, the Tallassee City Board of Education employed only single female teachers, and they were required to live in a teacherage. The board of education built two teacherages, one in East Tallassee, which is now a private residence, and another in West Tallassee, which was demolished in 1975. Shown here in this early 1940s photograph in East Tallassee on Alber Drive are, from left to right, the home of Robert E. Ledbetter (32 Alber Drive) and the East Tallassee Elementary School teacherage, a residence for unmarried female teachers. (Courtesy THPS.)

More than 2,500 Tallasseeans served in the armed forces during World War II. Company No. 46 of the Alabama State Guard was organized in 1946 in Tallassee to protect the home front. They drilled at the ballpark; most of them were high school students, ages 16 to 18. Pictured here in front of Tallassee High School are members of that unit, from left to right, (first row) Capt. William Frederick Dobbs, Jack McCullough, Wilson Patterson, and unidentified. The others are also unidentified. (Courtesy Frederica D. Melton.)

Nine

A SPIRITUAL SIDE

The people of Tallassee have always had a strong spiritual side. On August 2, 1852, the First Baptist Church was organized in a log house. In 1858, a one-room church was built, and it served the community until 1919, when a new church was built. In 1855, the Tallassee Methodist Church was established. Shown in 1889 are members of the First Baptist Church Singing School, which was organized by J. H. Norton, pastor. The building in the background is the 1858 church, which was used for 60 years until a new church was built in 1919. (Courtesy First Baptist Church.)

The East Tallassee Baptist Church was organized in 1899. In 1904, the congregation held its first service in this building, located at the corner of Central Avenue and Third Street. (Courtesy THPS.)

Shown here are members of the 1898 Tallassee Methodist Episcopal Church on King Street. (Courtesy THPS.)

This 20th-century view of the 1898 Tallassee Methodist Episcopal Church was published and distributed in the early 1900s by Dr. John William Dorough, a local physician. (Courtesy Jeff Parker.)

This view of the north side of King Street is taken from a postcard printed in Germany for the Bilbrey Studio in Tallassee. Pictured from left to right are the 1898 Methodist Episcopal Church, the B. B. Nelson–Dennis Redding house, the Robert Hill house, the Teacherage Annex–Lockwood house, the Crockett–Darrell Wilson house, and the Eubanks–James Patterson house. The postcard is postmarked June 11, 1909. (Courtesy Bennie Little.)

This c. 1900 photograph shows the old Watson Chapel Church and its members in the Red Hill community. (Courtesy Paula Eller Castleberry.)

Pictured here is a 1940s view of the East Tallassee Church of Christ on Powers Street in East Tallassee. (Courtesy THPS.)

This postcard shows the 1919 First Baptist Church (top) at the corner of James Street and South Dubois Street and the 1929 First United Methodist Church at the corner of Barnett Street and Jordan Avenue. (Courtesy Jeff Parker.)

Active in community life, many churches sponsored ball teams. Shown here is the East Tallassee Baptist Church baseball team. (Courtesy THPS.)

Pictured in 1925 on the east side of the 1898 Tallassee King Street Methodist Church are members of the Women's Society of Christian Service. Shown from left to right are (first row) Lucas Herren, Mary Herren Hayes, Maedee Dobbs, Maude Mathis, unidentified, and Mary Cliff Herren; (second row) Kate Burton, Myrtice Patterson, Ruth Noble, Kate Patterson, Ida Turrentine, Mary Elizabeth Dobbs, ? Kelley, Grace Harris, and Valeria Dubberly; (third row) Kirk Carr, Annie Bilbrey, Nancy Herren Holloway, ? Stanfield, Virginia Scott, unidentified, ? McGarr, three unidentified, and Nina Dubberly. (Courtesy Frederica D. Melton.)

Shown in this 1890s Bilbrey Studio photograph is the Baraca Class, a men's Sunday School class at the Tallassee First Baptist Church. Baraca comes from the Hebrew word *Berachah*, meaning blessing. (Courtesy First Baptist Church.)

Ten

THE "E" AWARD TOWN

On April 7, 1943, before a crowd of more than 7,500, the Tallassee Mills received the Army-Navy "E" Award from the U.S. government for excellence and efficiency in the production of war materials. The "E" Award was the highest honor the nation bestowed to those involved in war production. The Tallassee Mills earned the award again in 1944 and 1945. During World War II, the Tallassee Mills' wartime production began in December 1941. Holding the flag are, from left to right, Thomas Holmes Floyd, mill superintendent; unidentified; Lurline Leonard, smash hand-worker in weaving; J. W. Phillips, slubber tender in the card room; and Charles Stalnaker, truck driver. (Courtesy THPS.)

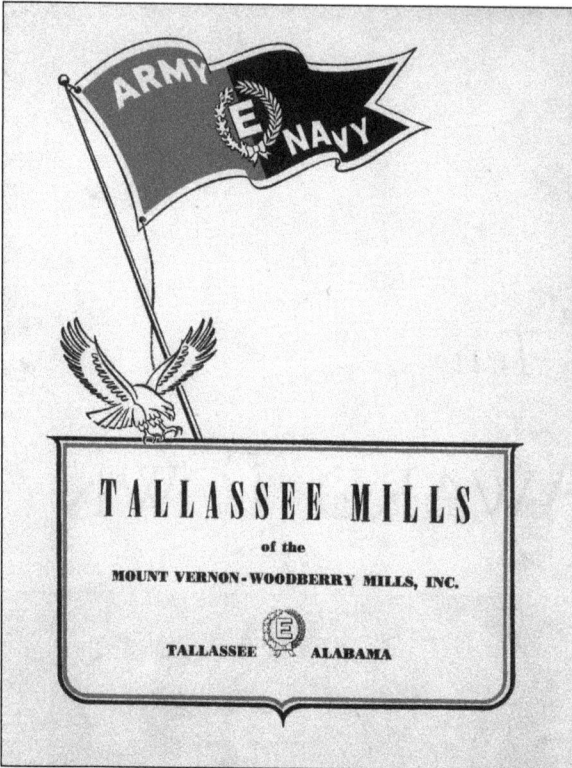

This official program was distributed to those who attended the ceremony on April 7, 1943, at the Tallassee Mills. (Courtesy THPS.)

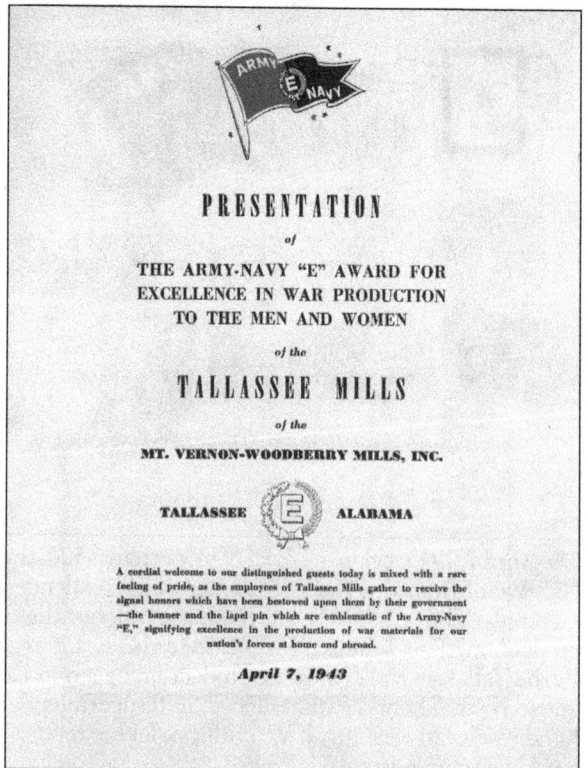

The second page of the official program at the Army-Navy "E" Award ceremony on April 7, 1943, in Tallassee formally proclaimed the "E" Award presentation. (Courtesy THPS.)

An official letter from the U.S. War Department announced the award's presentation. (Courtesy THPS.)

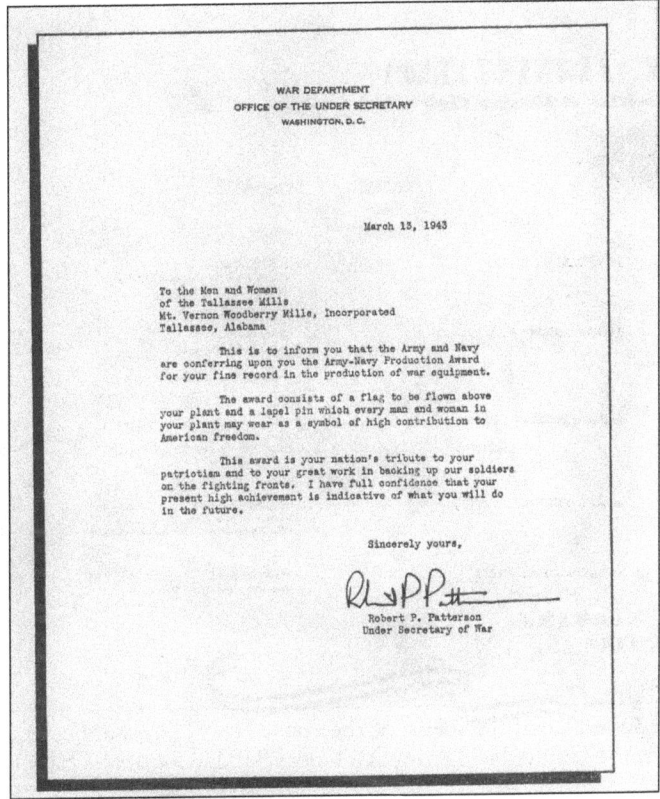

WAR DEPARTMENT
OFFICE OF THE UNDER SECRETARY
WASHINGTON, D.C.

March 13, 1943

To the Men and Women
of the Tallassee Mills
Mt. Vernon Woodberry Mills, Incorporated
Tallassee, Alabama

This is to inform you that the Army and Navy
are conferring upon you the Army-Navy Production Award
for your fine record in the production of war equipment.

The award consists of a flag to be flown above
your plant and a lapel pin which every man and woman in
your plant may wear as a symbol of high contribution to
American freedom.

This award is your nation's tribute to your
patriotism and to your great work in backing up our soldiers
on the fighting fronts. I have full confidence that your
present high achievement is indicative of what you will do
in the future.

Sincerely yours,

Robert P. Patterson
Under Secretary of War

Each worker received this Certificate of Appreciation and a small Army-Navy "E" lapel pin. During World War II, the Tallassee Mills employed 4,500 workers and operated three shifts. Each shift worked six days per week and supplied the armed forces with cotton duck for tents and cots, cotton drills, twine, and rope. (Courtesy THPS.)

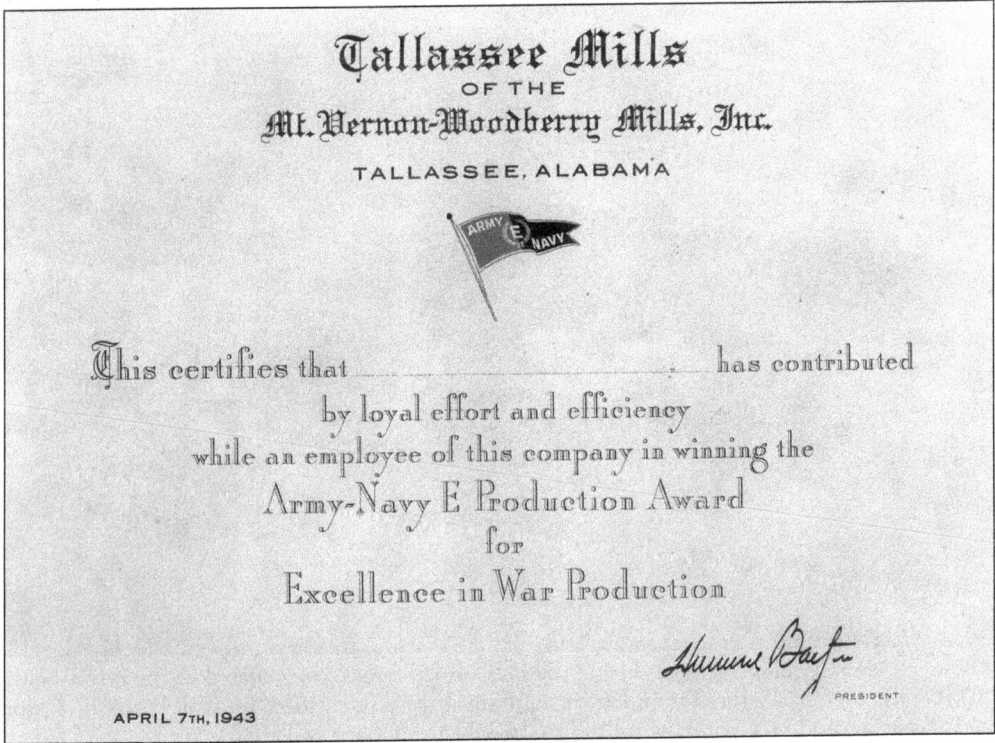

Tallassee Mills
OF THE
Mt. Vernon-Woodberry Mills, Inc.
TALLASSEE, ALABAMA

This certifies that _____ has contributed
by loyal effort and efficiency
while an employee of this company in winning the
Army-Navy E Production Award
for
Excellence in War Production

PRESIDENT

APRIL 7TH, 1943

Louise Dobbs, the soloist at the Army-Navy "E" Award ceremony, sang *America*, accompanied by the Gunter Field Army Air Corps Band. (Courtesy THPS.)

These five military officers, representing the U.S. armed forces, participated in the Army-Navy "E" Award program. Pictured from left to right are three unidentified, Lt. Col. Frank E. Taylor Jr., U.S. Army; and Lt. Com. Edwin Phillips, U.S. Navy. (Courtesy THPS.)

Some of the dignitaries who participated in the Army-Navy "E" Award ceremony are shown here, from left to right: unidentified; B. G. Stumberg, Tallassee Mills agent; John Ed Harris, vice president of Mount Vernon–Woodberry Mills; Thomas H. Floyd, Tallassee Mills superintendent; and unidentified. (Courtesy THPS.)

More than 7,500 individuals attended the Army-Navy "E" Award ceremony. In the background stand two of the four Tallassee Mills. On the left is the 1924 mill, built of concrete and steel; on the right is the 1897 mill, built of blue granite stone taken from the Tallapoosa River. Both of these mills are located in East Tallassee in Tallapoosa County. (Courtesy THPS.)

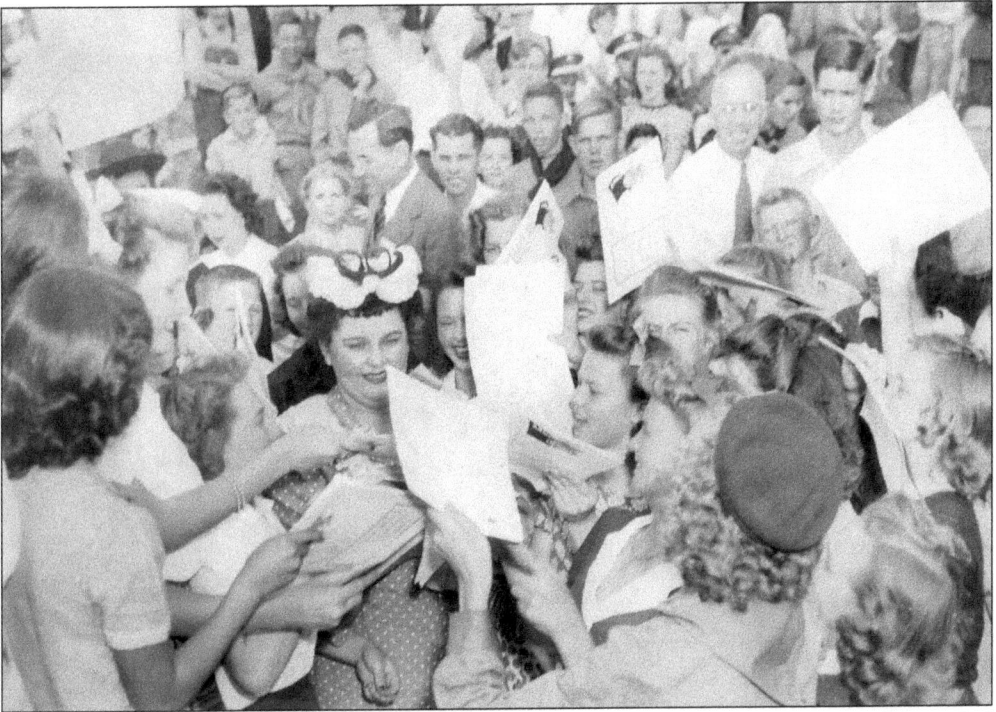

Louise Dobbs, the soloist at the Army-Navy "E" Award ceremony on April 7, 1943, is surrounded by admirers and autograph seekers. (Courtesy THPS.)

Lt. Com. Edwin Phillips, commanding officer of the Naval Training School at Alabama Polytechnic Institute (now Auburn University) in Auburn, Alabama, who presented the Army-Navy "E" pins, is surrounded by spectators at the April 7, 1943, event. (Courtesy THPS.)

The Gunter Field Army Air Corps Band from Montgomery, Alabama, presented a concert of patriotic music before and after the Army-Navy "E" Award ceremony on April 7, 1943. (Courtesy THPS.)

The Tallassee Red Cross chapter, which was organized during World War I, continued during World War II. During the 1940s, more than 100 volunteers served the Tallassee chapter under the leadership of Wilson Patterson, chairman. Pictured here in 1942 at the Red Cross hut on Barnett Street are, from left to right, Howard Golden, Virginia Noble Golden, and Virginia's mother, Ruth H. Noble. (Courtesy THPS.)

126

The Honor Roll Board, erected by the Tallassee Mills at the East Tallassee Mills, contained the names of all the mill workers who served in the armed forces during World War II. (Courtesy THPS.)

Spectators stand and watch the Army-Navy "E" Award ceremony. At the top of the photograph on the right is the Benjamin Fitzpatrick Bridge, which opened in 1940, spanning the Tallapoosa River and joining East and West Tallassee. (Courtesy THPS.)

Visit us at
arcadiapublishing.com

www.ingramcontent.com/pod-product-compliance
Lightning Source LLC
Chambersburg PA
CBHW050601110426
42813CB00008B/2421